"Working as a contractor refurbishing cruise ships in drydock in foreign ports, clearing brush and planting a vineyard on his Oregon acreage, 'urging' a kayak into the swift current of a river channel . . . these are a few of the scenes and subjects contained in this book of honest, authentic poems written by someone who has 'been there, done that.' Composed for the spoken voice, they read easily, in cadenced lines with the small felicities of expression that mark the work of a real craftsman. Above all, they are uncommonly interesting—vivid accounts of one man's sojourn on the planet."--Clemens Starck

"Reverberant, heart-catching, full of devotions and brightnesses, from 'First light / arching over the hemlocks' to a bearded carpenter playing Pachelbel's *Canon in D*, from sandals guarding the gates of a mosque in Marrakech to a daughter recovered from illness, Tim Applegate's poetry–clear, generous, insightful–is a treble bell, poem after poem rings true."--Melanie Green

"Applegate's wanderings of mind and geography lead us on a path that circles the globe. In clear open language, through narrative and image, we travel where: 'On certain mornings / the streets of Antigua are so tranquil / it's as if we could disappear in the silence / that hangs, like mist, over the town.' We meet outrigger canoes 'Five days north of Sydney. . . .' In passion '. . . the river reverses direction, flows back into itself. . . .' His work of refurbishing seagoing craft has taken him far and wide, eventually leading us back home, clearing field stones and creating a vineyard. *Blueprints* follows a wide trail, rich in musings."--Gary Lark

For Sue,
with appreciation for all
your fine poems.

December 2015

BLUEPRINTS

Poems by Tim Applegate

Acknowledgments

The author would like to thank the editors of the journals in which the following poems, some in slightly different versions, first appeared.

White Wall Review: Blueprints
The Connecticut River Review: Happiness; The Bomb Shelter
Wild Violet: Pinyons
Open Spaces: Shelter
The Tipton Journal: Mildred
Cloudbank: The Stagehand's Reply; Prime Rib
The Meadow: Faces
The Briar Cliff Review: Ink
Scrivener: Faulkner
The Blue Collar Review: Working the Ships; The Piano Player; Volcano
Chrysanthemum: Two Pairs of Sandals
Windfall: Stroke of Blue; Slocan Valley
Fault Lines: The Stanfields
Studio One: Hashim
Grasslimb Journal: Mornings in Antigua
Fox Cry Review: Snapshot
Ginger Hill: The Kayak
Cairn: The Magician
Moving Mountain: After Hiking Up Neahkahnie Mountain
Chagrin River Review: The Wheat Field; A Marriage; Clearcuts; The Leaves of the Maples
Drydock (Blue Cubicle Press, 2014): Working the Ships, A Plate of Tamales, The Piano Player, Volcano, The Contractors, Crew Bar, Stroke of Blue, The Stanfields, Blueprints, The Vineyard, The Coffee Fields, and Clearing the Brush

The author would like to thank Sandy Mason and Ruth F. Harrison at Turnstone Books, David LaBounty at Blue Cubicle Press, and the following writers for their careful reading of earlier drafts of the poems: Alison Apotheker, Barbara Drake, Michael McDowell, Amy Minato, Erik Muller, and Bill Siverly.

For Erik Muller

CONTENTS

I

II

III

IV

"A man's road back to himself is a return from his spiritual exile, for that is what a personal history amounts to—exile."

Saul Bellow, *The Actual*

I

BLUEPRINTS

Across Patton Valley this morning
pneumatic nail guns
punch holes in the air
as a crew of carpenters
frames a new home.

Like the carpenters, I study
my blueprints – Lorca today.

Reposition the ladder.

Climb.

CLEARING THE BRUSH

As I clear the brush choking the trees
that canopy our lower acre, I recall
Neruda's reference to those poets
whose language in old age gains a new
purity, a rustic simplicity, a paring down.

Clearing brush, pruning the azaleas, stopping
at Rudy's for a haircut when I drive
into town . . . This, then, is the paring down,
the great epic poem I once foolishly imagined
my life would be compressed into a few lines
of haiku. And no shame, no sadness, no
regret in that. The woman

first cherished thirty years ago
cherished even more now. The beautiful daughters
grown, freed, unleashed. And these gifts the world
keeps bestowing on us, bestowed on us, whether
we deserve them or not. First light
arching over the hemlocks. The weight of grapes
in the vineyard. Summer rain.

To be loved, Raymond Carver wrote

near the end: beloved. What else, then and now,

really mattered? To tumble in the arms

of another over the cliffs of sleep

into this clearing in the woods

where deer, once hidden by foliage,

now forage in full view.

HAPPINESS

Come fall, he planted two pear trees out
by the pond in the hope that one day
they would bear on their bony shoulders
the fruit of his grief.

But it doesn't work that way. The rains
come and go and the leaves skitter across the grass,
naming the days. Or the air turns blue with cold and
the pond freezes over and the boughs remain bare.

At a certain age, a poet tells him,
everything you write will be about loss, and he
recalls with a pang the year they all read
Meditation At Lagunitas on Caspersen Beach.

One evening when a harvest moon
rises in the kitchen window he glimpses, briefly,
happiness, an emotion he doesn't quite trust,
and probably shouldn't. Because

all the new thinking, Hass wrote,
is about loss. In this it resembles

all the old thinking.
He pictures the pear trees

out by the pond. How
he'll mulch, now that
it's spring, their beds.
How he'll prune their unruly branches.

PINYONS

On a wind-battered stretch of Oregon coastline
I stop the car to stand in the rain
and snap a photograph of a dwarf pine
which has – against what odds? – taken root
in a slab of granite
buried in the mud flats of the sea.

As I press my eye to the lens
I recall the pinyons that grew in the high
desert – stopping to photograph them – and begin
to hum the song the wind was singing
in the dry throats of those trees.

*   *

On the way home I stop to hum the river, to cast
its dark pools for trout. Then
my mother, unchanged by death, is
standing beside me, calm and attendant, watching

the silver fly arc through the air and land,
without a ripple, on the surface of the stream.

THE COIN

The Shan monks of Burma, who believed
that a man's soul was transported
across the River of Death, placed a coin
under the dead man's tongue
to pay the ferryman for his passage.

So save a coin for me.
A peso from Guadalajara
or a dirham from Marrakech.
Or better yet, one of the pennies
my sister and I buried in a jar
in the back yard of the house
in Terre Haute.

Dig a hole beneath the garden bench.
But hurry. The river
rises. The ferryman waits.

RIDING THE EMPIRE BUILDER HOME
FROM MY SISTER'S FUNERAL

In the prairie distance
a lamp burned in the window
of an isolated farmhouse,

but when the train passed by
the light went out.

Wind shivered in the grass,
then didn't.

SHELTER

Up above the tide pools and shell middens
the windy bluff the steep hillsides
I cross an old wooden bridge into stands
of high timber and in a clearing of cedars
stumble across an abandoned home someone's
dream of coastal shelter fallen into disuse
this house this land these beams and rafters
lying in the sun this chimney
collapsing into rubble one brick at a time
these broken windows scattered in the weeds
some of the slender mullions
still holding shards of glass and their jagged
reflections a patch of sky or a knot of branches
or perhaps for the briefest moment the flight
of a hawk as the front door
of an abandoned home swings open
to let the fog pass through
the evening light the lost voices . . .

FISHING WITH MY MOTHER AT DIETZ LAKE

Since you were too squeamish
to bait your own hook, I baited it
for you, threading the worm through twice
so it wouldn't squirm off at the first nibble.

Slinging our lines into a finger-shaped cove,
we unfolded lawn chairs near the edge
of the water where later, when the autumn
air chilled, the sun slipped behind a belt of
beech trees on the opposite bank as
our bobbers bobbed, cattails shivered, your
rod bent and trembled
with the sudden weight of a fish . . .

In memory, the photograph
is sepia, mother and son sitting side by side
while something dark – a carp
or a gar – slides past them into the murky
depths of a future which, in my boyhood, in
that time of relative innocence, remained
unfathomable, undiscovered, still submerged.

THE BOMB SHELTER

In the summer of 1962, at the height of the Cuban missile crisis, Sally Evinger had a bomb shelter installed in her back yard to protect her loved ones on the Day of Flame, and one morning her son Johnny and I decided to stock the shelves with enough supplies (kerosene lanterns, Spaghetti-Os, Tang) to sustain us all during the forthcoming nuclear winter, which was projected to last for the next five hundred years.

Johnny went to Vietnam, and when he returned he was placed in a military hospital where a doctor in a white smock asked him to describe his dreams. The rice paddies at sunrise are beautiful, Johnny replied, and then all hell breaks loose. The authorities granted him leave to attend my wedding, and in the photographs of that joyous occasion he's the one wearing Bib overalls and carrying a battered guitar, like Woody Guthrie.

The day Johnny died the rumors began: drugs, drink, Agent Orange. I woke my daughter and told her we were going to the beach. I was under the impression that the sun and the sea would anneal my sorrow, the fierce heat dull my pain, but that didn't happen. Later, when I described how Johnny and I used to hop freights across town and shoot rats down at the dump and sleep in a bomb shelter in the blast zone, Kerstin grew quiet and pensive, the way she did when I read her stories about exotic adventures in far-off lands.

MILDRED

Father dies.
Then the insurance man with one glass eye
comes to court Mother, who smiles through
the haze of her grief, a thousand miles away.

I'm twelve, thirteen, and these are the years
of the house call, Dr. Miklozek drifting down
the hallway with a syringe
of morphine for Mildred.

I didn't like you, she says. I'm nineteen,
twenty. For years I didn't really like you.

*   *

Six men carry my father's coffin
across a barren hillside (no, there were crosses, a
sea of white crosses) and now gunshots – military
gunshots – clear the birds from their winter nests.

That night I dream of riders in the rain, a plague
of ravens, a man bending down

to whisper something to Mildred, who
isn't listening. He hands her a flag.

*   *

I'm marching against the war in Vietnam
when a few jocks from a nearby high school

scatter the ranks of the protestors
with baseball bats.

A girl I've known since I was a child
doubles over on the sidewalk, taking it.

*   *

When the monk on the screen
goes up in flames, in saffron flames,

Mildred's hand inches
across the sofa, briefly clutches mine.

OVER THE MOUNTAIN

facing the blank page
over the mountain
mountains

     lost in the mountains
     at dusk, that first
     faint star

black ice this morning
on Bald Peak Road
I press the snooze button twice

     losing my temper
     outside, pellets
     of frozen rain

the koi pond frozen over . . .
all morning
your silence

     two trails
     over the mountain
     the choices we made

re-reading *Riprap*
moon over Cold Mountain rises,
in my window, over Bald Peak

     spring thaw
     unlocks the pond
     in the firs, the first goldfinch

two trails
over the mountain
only one leads home

THE PATH

The day the sky rained poplar leaves months out of season I was sitting on the back deck reading the prose poems of Robert Bly when the yellow leaves began to float down from the mountain a few at first and then many not cracked and curled like the dead leaves of autumn but smooth and glossy and almost weightless and as the wind rose on the back slope scattering and lifting the leaves I considered the word enchantment and said it out loud letting the weight of it roll against my tongue and when I went inside to turn on the lamps I noticed that some of the leaves had skittered across the deck and blown into the house and now shaped against the gray weave of the carpet a kind of path.

II

WORKING THE SHIPS

*"A breach was made and the basin quickly filled
with water. Then the water was pumped out so
that the ships were suspended in air."*
--Shen Kuo, *Dream Pool Essays, 1088*

All night long a crane lifts containers onto Deck 9
of the cruise ship we're refurbishing. A hundred
rolls of carpet. Tiffany lamps for the casino.
Ceramic tiles for the spa.

On the second morning Doug and I
cobble together a spray booth with blue tarps,
a coil of rope and a roll of duct tape. When we
run out of lacquer, Kati Selfridge
finds a local supplier down by the docks.

The diesel mechanics are Aussies: hard drinkers,
expert calibrators, tellers of extravagant tales.
The tile setters are from Michigan, or Palermo,
or Peru. The bartender's Malaysian,
by way of Bangladesh.

Working the ships the world over to pay off
a mortgage back home. The flights in, the flights
out, the work, the rest, the meals, the camaraderie,

the stress. Caught in the whirl and only later, in
memory, these postcards, these snapshots

of an itinerant life. A tavern in Sydney where I
recited, over pints of Guinness, a poem by Frost.
Sunrise over Kauai from ten miles out. Walking
down the rainy streets of Gibraltar, the same
cobbled streets my father walked down sixty years
ago, on his way home from the war . . .

A PLATE OF TAMALES

On the upper deck of the Princess Ruby
I execute my half of one of those elaborate
choreographed handshakes – high five and a fist
bump followed, at last, by a manly thump
to the chest – with Mario, an apprentice welder
who up until three weeks ago had never flown
on a plane or set foot on a seagoing vessel.

Now at the end of a drydock
he's sailing the southern Med.

Disoriented by the ship's complex maneuvers
leaving Gibraltar, Mario points at the white
coastline sliding past us and says, "What is that,
Teem?" "That," I reply, "is Spain." And now it's
my turn to point back across the shimmering
channel. "And that," I tell him, "is Morocco."

For a long time Mario remains silent, perhaps
imagining how one day he'll return to the border
town in Texas where he was born to explain
all this, over a plate of tamales, to his father.

"Morocco, Papa. Spain."

VOLCANO

Five days north of Sydney
we spot a dozen outrigger canoes
gliding across the smooth waters that lie
in the shadow of a smoldering volcano, a steady
plume of smoke billowing
from its central crater as if, at any minute,
the entire mountain might explode.

It's an otherworldly moment, a crew of contractors
on a modern cruise ship recording, with the latest
digital technology, this strange flotilla – one native
per craft – out fishing their aboriginal waters
for yellowfin tuna and horseshoe crab.

*   *

While the Filipino bartender describes,
rhapsodically, the pork *mechado* his mother
used to cook for him when he was a boy, T, nine
years on the ships, announces not for the first
time his intention to relocate to Vegas to work,
union, on new homes. Nicholson is looking
at land in Guatemala. Roger, tired of painting

steel, is moving to Martha's Vineyard
to apprentice in Italian tile.

Everyone is going somewhere, to do
something else. And in six months we'll all
meet again on yet another foreign vessel
anchored in the harbor of yet another
foreign sea, for we're all tiny cogs

in the great turning wheel
of ship refurbishment, the carpenters
and electricians, the welders and wood
refinishers, the common anonymous workers
the passenger rarely sees.

*   *

I raise my hands high in the air
until one of the natives

waves, in salutation,
the paddle of his canoe.

THE PIANO PLAYER

The Grand Princess, Bahamas

On the final day of the Freeport drydock workers roll a grand piano onto the dais of the remodeled atrium, and that night, as I store our coatings – lacquers, sanding sealers, polyurethanes – in a gang box, I hear the first faint notes of Pachelbel's *Canon in* D.

Assuming that the piano player has arrived onboard to fine-tune his instrument for the guests who will stream onto the ship tomorrow morning, I lock the gang box and step into the atrium only to discover that the musician is Eric, a quiet, bearded carpenter known not for his musical talent but for his ability to cut precise, beveled lengths of mahogany trim on a table saw.

Jimmy unplugs his router. Frank spools his measuring tape. The rags of the cleaners pause in mid-swipe . . . Until Eric, with a modest flourish, brings the canon to a close and rises from his bench, blinking in astonishment at our spontaneous applause.

CREW BAR

Another spring, another city, another ship: at dusk
the massive high-rise apartment blocks of Singapore
disappear in the watery distance as
the Princess Dawn sails, under power, into open sea.

I meet Nicholson in the crew bar. Halfway
through the job, halfway home, many
of the workers are tense, worn out, and quick
tempered. But like me, Nicholson's convinced
that the perfect antidote to labor is literature, so
we order a round of Heinekens and settle in
to discuss Whitman, Hemingway, and Thoreau.

Behind us, a sudden raised voice and a brief
vehement argument as Andre – an amateur boxer
and a part-time electrician – storms out of the room.

"If Whitman was here," I proclaim, "he would sing
the praises of these rough-hewn workingmen
sailing the seven seas for their daily bread," but
Nicholson's not so sure. "There's enough
testosterone on this ship," he mutters darkly,
"to start World War Three."

*   *

I like to imagine Whitman in Los Angeles
singing the praises of Andre.
Sunday morning, the gym empty except

for the boxer who circles the heavy bag
hanging from its chain, launching a jab
or a hook, circling, stalking, lithe as a leopard,
sweat now beading his smooth black skin.

Andre climbs into the ring, bouncing on
the balls of his feet, shadow-boxing
the Texas redneck who muttered a racial slur
in the crew bar of the Princess Dawn the day
it left Singapore, his concentration so pure,

so complete he fails to notice the old poet
with the long gray beard perched on a stool
in the corner of the gym, dark
eyes beneath the brim of a slouch hat
tracking the welterweight's every move.

THE CONTRACTORS

On their way out of town two contractors
stop at a local market to buy a wedge
of brie, sliced discs of salami, a baguette.

They consider the red grapes (imported, pricey),
and the mangoes (bruised, overripe), before
settling on tangerines. A jar of olives. A Beaujolais.

At the hotel
they tally the hours they worked that week,
and add travel time. Check their cell phones

for messages from home, swim laps
in the pool, arrange a shuttle
to the airport for the following day.

Now that the gang box they store their tools in
has been offloaded onto a container vessel
bound for LA, they have an entire day and night

to do whatever they want, though it takes a while
to decompress from the rigors of the job. After
lunch, one strolls the grounds with a digital

camera snapping, in sequence, hibiscus,
frangipani, and a breadfruit tree. The other writes
poems, in the shade of a banana palm, in Tahiti.

STROKE OF BLUE

When you work on a ship in drydock
the sea shimmers on the horizon, a stroke of blue
along the outer edge of a vast industrial canvas,
a tangle of cranes, forklifts, men in yellow
hardhats, pallets of marine varnish, coils of rope.

For two weeks the water
glitters in the distance, catches your eye.
You might call this symbolic – a glimpse of
freedom – but that would be trite. For what
the sea represents is simpler than that: passage,
a paycheck, the end of the job.

Eventually the floodgates inch open
and the ship begins to tremble,
to shudder, to sway.

You join the others up top. Wind tousles
your hair. Someone hands you a Heineken.
Someone else points out, at the mouth of
Victoria Harbor, the Fairmont Empress Hotel.

Now your course is due north, back to a berth

in Vancouver, a shuttle to the airport,

the short flight home over

a stroke of blue water, slash of dry land.

A GAME OF DOMINOS

Rincon, Puerto Rico

In Rincon I cross the town plaza where two old men,
in the shadow of the church of Santa Rosa de Lima,
play a game of dominos, gnarled fingers carefully
placing each tile in position.

Off the coast, the cruise ship I've been working on
for the last two weeks bears north, bound
for the Bahamas, the sky clear today in this season
of hurricanes, in this season of storms.

      *   *

Past the domino tables, the empty band shell,
a food cart featuring *mofongo* and *bacalao*,
I slip inside the church: orderly pews, modest
altar, the hush of reverence.

Is this where the parishioners gathered
when the hurricanes of '67 and '79 swept
across their island? Is this where, whispering
their prayers, they rode out those storms?

33

*   *

In 19th Century rural England dominos
were used to settle boundary disputes,
but these two players have something less
momentous in mind. They shuffle the tiles, tally

their scores, place friendly wagers. With money
in their pockets and time on their hands
they have the good sense to bask in the light
that floods the plaza, in a bowl of the *bacalao*,
shimmering with salty cod, their mothers
used to cook for them when they were boys.

*   *

As they finish the *bacalao* and resume
their game, I picture myself in ten years,
suddenly as old as they are, sitting on
a park bench at dusk in a different town plaza,
feeding the pigeons or reading a book
of John Berryman's poems. Soon the dark
will make whatever I do next

seem inconsequential, and yet the simplest
acts will offer me solace, just as a game
of dominos once offered those two men joy.
In the fading light, in the gathering shadows,
I'll feed the pigeons, I'll read Berryman's poems.

III

AFTER THE MOVIE

After the movie the couple stopped at a shop
for ice cream, then at a tavern across the street
for a pint of beer. Later, as they strolled
home, the man was unusually quiet – the film

had disturbed him – but the woman
was content, perhaps even happy. The night
was clear and the lights in all the tidy houses
made her feel, at least for now, safe.

Because you could get lost in a college town too,
in the ivy. You could drink too much too often.
You could sleep with strangers. You could gouge
the walls of your marriage with the chisel of your wit.

And in between those times
you could go to the movies. The screen darkens.
There's that moment when the world seems perfect.
She grabs hold of her husband's hand.

THE STAGEHAND'S REPLY

At the Musical Arts Center in Bloomington
Jeff Thompson and I built stage sets
for upcoming productions. Chekov's parlor.
The playground in *West Side Story*.
A balcony for Juliet.

In between acts we rolled the new flats
onto the stage as quietly as possible, and rolled
the others away. When the lights came up
and the actors took their bows, we stood
in the wings, applauding.

After final performances
we joined the cast at a tavern across the street
for the closing-night party. Music, stories,
a burst of laughter, and round
after round of drinks.

Yet even at the tavern, we each
had a role to play. Jeff and I
were the stagehands, two kids
working their way through college
building props for performers like these.

Uncle Vanya polished his fob watch. King Lear
made a move on Eliza Doolittle. And on one
particularly memorable evening Blanche Dubois
leaned over my table
in a low-cut dress, purring words.

But I couldn't hear her. The music was too loud,
the lighting too harsh, and in the sudden glare
of Blanche's attention I froze, unable
to imagine the next
line of dialogue, the stagehand's reply.

FACES

On the wall above the urinal someone
had written, in fine cursive script, *God Is Dead*,
as if to prove that this was, indeed, a college
tavern. Peanut shells on the floor, spilled beer
on the tables, a heated debate over the relative
merits of the novels of Jean Genet.

One night a wife walked out on her husband.
They had been discussing a movie, one of
John Cassavetes' *cinema verite* meditations on
marital despair, when the woman finished
her drink, set the empty glass down on the bar,
and calmly strolled out of the tavern.

Relationships were impossible but the town
itself was lovely. Autumn. Fallen leaves, a
gibbous moon, the halo of a streetlamp. One night
a wife stepped into Showalter Fountain, soaking
her shoes. She didn't particularly care. God
was dead and the water was cool

and as I stood over that urinal, wondering where
she'd gone, I recalled the name of the Cassavetes
film we'd been discussing. *Faces.* Seymour Cassel
alone at the top of the stairs. In a faithless world,
Cassel must have thought, anything
could happen, and probably would.

A MARRIAGE

He wanted to clear the hillside

so the water from the spring

could flow free again

could pool at the bottom into a bog

where he would plant comfrey

to make a poultice

for the fingers she pricked

filling pail after pail

with berries from the vines

he kept yanking

by their taproots

from the ground.

THE LEAVES OF THE MAPLES

Words fail, or the autumn light, bruised
by rain clouds, fades too early, or
their lovemaking fails, it's too passionate,
it's not passionate enough, her mind
is elsewhere, his body right there . . . As they
rise in the gloom of dusk, the man dressing
quickly now, impatient to return
to his file of poems, to the words
that lend his life shape and balance
when nothing else seems to, writing
in the shadows while the woman
at the bedroom window
watches the leaves of the maples
fall soundlessly to ground.

TWO PAIRS OF SANDALS

Marrakech

across the morning rooftops
a muezzin calls the prayer . . .
and a sparrow answers

       tourists stream across the plaza
       a single dirham
       in the beggar's palsied hand

at the end of the avenue
two pairs of sandals
guard the gates of the mosque

PAUL STRAND IN MOROCCO

As the doors of the bus hiss open, Strand steps out into high desert glare: Tahanoute, a Berber village south of Marrakech. It's 1962 and the world has just witnessed, on its sixteen-inch screens, the first manned space flight, but here on the dusty plateaus of central Morocco the photographer has ventured back into a different century, a different time. Women in white burkas stream into the village while merchants set up stalls along the knee wall that encircles the plaza. Market day. Figs and melons, scarves stained crimson in the dye souks of Casablanca, pyramids of spice.

Behind his tripod Strand waits for the light to clear and flatten over the High Atlas, for the shadows of the peaks to drift out across the plain. Then he crouches over his camera, pressing his eye to the lens and framing the composition – just as he framed the fishnets of Janitzio or the ramparts of Cortona or a Spanish broom – because it is all connected, all one thing, the work of a lifetime. He squeezes the shot.

Raised voices – the universal language of barter – float above the square as Strand caps the lens and joins his wife in the market. At first curious, and camera shy, the Berbers now ignore him. He shuffles past the stalls, sampling the delicacies, before stopping at one of the braziers to point at a roasted pigeon he then eats, honoring custom, with the fingers of his left hand.

HASHIM

Essaouira

A feral cat, pale as smoke, paws at a fishbone
wedged into the rocks at the edge of the harbor
where the fishermen clean their daily catch.

At his window, Hashim watches the cat
slink away and disappear in the shadows
of the ramparts. Then he closes the curtain
and turns back to his bowl of tagine, cup
of mint tea, book of ancient verse.

Tomorrow, they say, the wind will rise like wrath
and build towering walls of water,
but Hashim is unafraid because he knows
that everything was written long ago.
Written in the sand, carved in stone, slashed
into the bark of the argan trees.

He falls asleep whispering the familiar verses.
In his dream a blue boat
breaks loose from its mooring and floats
out to sea, the fog's only color.

SLOCAN VALLEY

British Columbia

SANDON

In 1898, at the height of the silver boom, there
were twenty-nine hotels here including the Rico
where a suddenly wealthy prospector could dine
on broasted oysters, beef medallions,
and flutes of champagne.

Twenty-eight saloons, two newspapers
and enough brothels to satisfy
the randiest young man.

Now a different kind of wind – song
of the dry claim – blows through Sandon
where, during the long and harsh
winters, the population is twelve.

THE SHUSWAP

On the aboriginal land
their ancestors hunted and fished for
two thousand years, the children of the Shuswap
still hang their salmon in strips above

the smokehouse fires, the tender meat
charred tonight for fritters.

Stories of the old days, the old ways
over baskets of bannock, venison sausages,
beds of lentils and cream.

ALONG THE EAGLE RIVER

Every few miles another cedar flume – flume
that washed the silver down
the hillsides – collapses under the weight
of a pauper's dream.

In the shadow of the train trestle
a trout rises to the surface
to nip at a fisherman's yellow fly.
Rises into this moment, and
into this moment disappears.

THE COFFEE FIELDS

On the map on the wall of the restaurant he owns
I show Antonio the places in Guatemala
my wife and I plan to visit. Antigua.
Lake Atitlan. Tikal.

When he talks about his country
Antonio's voice is the rain that falls on
the coffee fields his family worked in when he
was a boy. "When we walked to the fields
in the morning we sang. We didn't
have a dime, but we sang."

A week later a rickety bus rattles up the green
shoulder of a mountain. At the top, Sue
points out the window and says *there's Antonio,*
indicating a boy crossing a coffee field, carrying
a burlap bag, possibly singing.

MORNINGS IN ANTIGUA

At the psych ward, my wife tends patients
who have forgotten who they are.
Like the song in the shell their faint,
windy voices, their hollow stares.

Picking at her lasagne, she insists
that when she looks at those patients
she doesn't see us one day, but
I'm not sure I believe her.

We fly to Guatemala, climb the volcano,
kayak the *isletas*, share a plate of
quesadillas at the Rainbow Café.
On certain mornings the streets of Antigua

are so tranquil it's as if we could disappear in
the silence that hangs, like mist, over
the town. But we don't. I nudge her awake
so we can take our coffee in the courtyard

where the orchids in the vases, defying
the season, continue to bloom.

ON THE OCKLAWAHA

Around the campfire, Michael Gardiner and I
were finishing our dinner when we heard it,
the unmistakable rattle of a pickup crawling along
the grassy track that skirts that section of river, in
the middle of nowhere, late on a Sunday night.
Instinctively I grabbed my hatchet and stood up.
The pickup stopped. Two men stepped out.

And now thirty years later when I wake in the dark
remembering that night on the Ocklawaha
I understand, for the first time, that it isn't the gator
on the bank or the riffles that threatened to topple
our canoe that frightens me. It isn't the sudden
squall in the slot canyon or the funnel cloud over
the valley or the fresh bear scat I stumbled across
once hiking up an alpine peak. It isn't even

the faint shadow on the x-ray or the persistent
spasms in my lower back that wakes me tonight.
It's the memory of how, when those two men
climbed out of their pickup, instead of lifting
a hand in greeting or offering them a beer,
I grabbed the nearest weapon.

SNAPSHOT

As I pause on the lip of a cliff
overlooking Bryce Canyon, my wife,
focusing the camera, says *pretend
you're falling, the way you used to.*

When we were young.
Before we found out what it felt like
to fall that far, hit that hard, spend
years nursing the bruises.

THE WHEAT FIELD

What happened in the wheat field?

    I heard the engine of a small plane sputter,

    then fail.

What did you do?

    I ran toward the fire, toward the flames.

What happened in the wheat field?

    A young girl, a child really, spoke in tongues.

And what did that sound like?

    A word-song. One part gospel, one part jazz.

What do you think she was saying?

    That a dying man must accept, even embrace,

    his terrible thirst.

What happened in the wheat field?

    After the fire was put out, horses gathered

    near the wreckage, no longer afraid.

Is all of this true?

    It's my interpretation of the truth, my

memory,

    what I saw that day.

What did you see?

    A child talking in tongues.

And what did that sound like?

    A river of words. A lineage.

A lineage?

> The stories we tell our children. What we
>
> pass on.

What happened in the wheat field?

> The pilot walked away from
>
> the plane, unharmed.

A miracle.

> No. Not that.

What then?

> Chance. An accident. A roll of
>
> the cosmic dice.

What happened in the wheat field?

> A small plane went down. There were
>
> some horses. The pilot walked away.

IV

THE GOLFER

At the end of the round the golfer keeps walking. Past the 18th green where the rest of the foursome stop to tally their scores. Past the parking lot's orderly row of Toyotas. Past the arched clubhouse windows gleaming in the afternoon sun.

In the upper meadow a sough of wind and the cry of a kestrel. Soon it will grow dark and the trail, if it rains, slippery. But for now the path is dry. As he climbs the next ridge and pauses at the top to look down on the golf course, the greens as small as stamps, the fairways like the links in a chain that no longer connects him to the world he's left behind.

INK

for Margaret Chula

And then one evening
I lit the stub of a candle, brewed
a small pot of tea,
and tipped my brush
with ink, the way I'd been taught
by certain masters.

The template
was modesty, those poems
that held, in their tiny fingers,
leaves, and wind.

Eventually the sun
would reappear in that kitchen window
but not before my brush
finally imagined, in a few
simple strokes, the black
whip of a river

between pines.

FAULKNER

How like the moon
in its oak

these barn boards
chinked with summer light.

He must have thought
even this, this single petal

driven through
a fallen timber vital.

Soon it was over:
spilled whiskey

in its aisle
of dust.

TRUSTING YOUR TOOLS

As if to prove the old maxim that bad things
happen in threes, the Vietnam poem turns
into a diatribe and dies on the page. The sauce
for the chicken fricassee scorches the skillet.
Then the power blinks off in the middle
of the night and I wake to winter, snow falling
like confetti from the sky.

You have to trust your tools, a carpenter
once told me: meter and metaphor, sauce pan
and garlic press, and now in the growing cold
the ax that splits the cedar, the wheelbarrow
that hauls the firewood up the hillside, even
the failed poem I crush
into a ball and slide under

a pyramid of kindling in the woodstove.
When I light a match,
the poem flares up like napalm,
igniting my pyre of wood.

CLEARCUTS

In the foothills above Patton Valley this morning
the clearcuts are buried
under a foot of new snow, last night's rain
freezing in the upper elevations
while the lower hillsides remain stained
in the earth tones of those early impressionists
who concluded that in an age of photography
realism was obsolete – that no matter
how skilled the artisan, an image on canvas
would never equal, in clarity,
that same image on film – and so
portrayed, instead, the idea of essence: the lilies
in a pond or the trees in a forest
even when those trees are toppled in clearcuts
buried, this morning, under a foot of new snow.

THE WAVE

"I left them all behind, blackberrying in the sun."
--Virginia Woolf, *Mrs. Dalloway*

At dawn the flame of the candle

flickers once, paling, briefly,

the woman's left hand. Outside, a horse

canters across a bridge, a bell

swings in its silver tower, the river

burrows deep in its own reflection.

And yet here, when her quill pen

loops across paper, it's easy

to imagine that ink is the potion

that will save the woman's life.

Finished, she eases opens the curtains,

watches a neighbor's dog – a Labrador – lope

down the sidewalk, the edge

of the sun appear, without warning,

over London's grey walls, the river

the same river, the town the same town,

this world, this moment, this now the same
now that keeps singing in the same insistent
voice she must have heard that day, stepping
into the wave.

CERULEAN BLUE

for my daughter Molly

And so you woke, after illness,
from the darkness of fever
to a day painted by
one of those Flemish masters
who understood that a wave of light
spilling through a kitchen window
is not measured by its radiance
but by the shadows it sketches
in the corners of the room, just
as they understood that when
the buxom peasant rises from her churn
to fling open that window
it isn't the strength of the light
but the depth of the pigment
that startles us: color of
memory, sky of childhood, cerulean blue.

TURNING SIXTY

"I'm glad I'll look when I'm old
Like a gypsy dusha hauling milk"
--Carolyn Forche, *The Morning Baking*

One night years ago, in a blur
of bourbon and self-pity,
I complained to a friend
that I had accomplished nothing.

"But you're still a young man," she
reassured me. Meaning I still had a chance
to put down this pen
and do something useful.

And maybe she was right, maybe writing poems
is nothing more than a man in a mirror
contemplating the attrition of time
even when, this morning, he ignores

the baffled scowl on his face
to consider, instead, a world
where gypsy dushas haul pails of milk
along the banks of the Vah River in Slovakia.

PRIME RIB

If you want to be considered a serious writer these days you must avoid, at all costs, sentimentality. So I'm not going to tell you how I finished the prime rib last night by smoking it over a bed of apple wood which had soaked all day in a bowl of warm water or how the smell of that wood reminded me of the afternoon I strolled through an orchard in southern Indiana with the first girl I ever loved. I'm not going to tell you about the horse I used to feed windfall apples to in Florida either, or the Brittany spaniel that liked to lie in the sun while I pruned out own modest orchard of fruit-bearing trees, and please, don't even get me started on my Aunt Deej's apple cobbler. What I will tell you is that our dinner guests were enthusiastic about the prime rib, one even claiming it the finest he had ever tasted, though I wonder now if he really meant what he said or if the smell of that charred wood triggered his own flood of primal memories, which combined with a vintage Cabernet might transform the most stoic guest into the kind of sentimental fool the rest of us, who yearn to be serious writers, pretend not to be.

THE MAGICIAN

Once, when the magician opened his fist
a dove appeared, or a spray of roses.
Little white bird blinked and blinked,
astonished to find itself
in that dark auditorium
and not in the branches of a tree.

As the moving van
backs out of my neighbor's driveway
and the faces of the children
press up against the windows of their car,
I lift a hand and open my fist, releasing
a dove, or roses.

THE KAYAK

for Sue

Beauty is so brief: a child
running through summer hayfields,
a blue iris, chevrons of geese.

And now dusk, like so many
dusks before it . . . Even in Kyoto, Basho wrote,
I long for Kyoto.

* *

At daybreak
I urge a kayak into the slender channel, the river's
swift current, holding steady, bearing west.
How many times

have I sought the quiet pleasures of solitude
only to yearn for the moon in the window, the pale
curve of your wrist or shoulder
on bed sheets?

* *

Late on a stormy, wind-tossed evening
I finish Sam Hamill's *Gratitude*, a book
so large-hearted my first reaction is shame.

What else makes us fully human
but the capacity to suffer love?

"What you give away is yours forever," Hamill
writes, so I give you this: a vow,
a blue iris, petals of rain.

*　　*

I want to turn the clocks back, to recapture
certain moments I cannot even name.

A cry of passion. A flight of egrets.
The wave of light
which will always, in my mind, be Sarasota.

*　　*

Anchored to the rhythm of the sea, the river
reverses direction, flows back into itself

the way I want to flow back into
our bodies, our lives.

And yet when I bank the kayak
in a slow circle home
it suddenly occurs to me that what I
wanted – love and rivers and poems – is what I have.

It could be this simple: at
the end of day, in gratitude, my small bow.

AFTER HIKING UP NEAHKAHNIE MOUNTAIN I STOP AT A NEARBY TAVERN FOR A PINT OF BEER

The guy on the next barstool is wearing camo. Hat,
jacket, pants – the whole nine yards. He's talking
about his right to bear arms, and when he inquires in
a friendly, conversational manner what kind of guns
I happen to own to protect what is rightfully mine, I
reply that I don't own any. I tell him I live
in the country and I'm not too worried about it. When
I leave for work in the morning, I don't
even lock my doors!

He stares at me hard, aghast. What is it you do, fella,
he growls, for a livin'? So I answer, I'm a poet, a
choice of vocation that leaves Camo Man speechless,
and without further ado he grabs his bottle of Bud
and marches off to the other end of the bar.

Which is unfortunate. If he stayed, I could have
shown him my new poem about the hike up
Neahkahnie Mountain, the one that describes
how when you reach the peak the clouds
break open and it's all right there: Wheeler,
the Nehalem River, Tillamook Bay . . .

THE STANFIELDS

Like many other families of the time,
my mother's English ancestors were named
for the work they performed, clearing stones
and boulders from the neighboring fields
so the local farmers – landowners – could
plant their crops.

Years ago my cousin Raymond traced
the Stanfields back to the Norman invasion
of 1066, but as I clear our upper acre to plant
a small family vineyard this morning,
little, it seems, has changed. The sun rises
over a tapestry of farms. At the bottom
of the hill a rooster crows, which wakes
the dogs, who start barking.

And as the ghosts of my ancestors
gather in the shade of a nearby maple
to light their pipes and comment on my
progress, I unearth stone after stubborn stone
with a mattock, a shovel, and my hands.

THE VINEYARD

for Barbara Drake

At the end of day I measure the last post,
drill quarter-inch holes, fasten clamps
to the wires that will bear, at harvest,
the weight of the fruit. And now two rows
of Pinot Noir are staked in the ground, next
to two rows of Riesling.

*   *

Then the wind picks up and I pause
among vines, lost in the past . . .

Working the ships again, this one seven days
out of Sydney. A quiet morning, the sea calm,
the wind a whisper. I'm having coffee with
Aussie Dave, who describes the vineyards
north of Adelaide, in the Clare Valley, known
for its excellent Shiraz.

*   *

What a Buddhist once taught me is that
the work, if work is what you choose
to call this, is never really done.

So I tighten the fruiting wire, string mesh
to keep the deer out, write a poem
for Barbara about grapes.

Tim Applegate's poems, essays, and short fiction appear in the *Florida Review*, *The South Dakota Review*, *Lake Effect*, and *The Briar Cliff Review* among many others. He is the author of the collections *At the End of Day* (Traprock Books) and *Drydock* (Blue Cubicle Press). His novel *Fever Tree* will be published by Amberjack Publishing in 2016. He lives in the Willamette Valley of western Oregon.

Made in the USA
Charleston, SC
16 December 2015